forever ell

19 Ella Fitzgerald Classics

© 2007 by Faber Music Ltd
First published in 1997 by International Music Publications Ltd
International Music Publications Ltd is a Faber Music company
3 Queen Square, London WC1N 3AU
Production: Sadie Cook
Cover by Watkiss Studios Limited
Printed in England by Caligraving Ltd
All rights reserved

ISBN10: 0-571-52390-0
EAN13: 978-0-571-52390-0

To buy Faber Music publications or to find out about the full range of titles available,
please contact your local music retailer or Faber Music sales enquiries:

Faber Music Ltd, Burnt Mill, Elizabeth Way, Harlow, CM20 2HX England
Tel: +44(0)1279 82 89 82   Fax: +44(0)1279 82 89 83
sales@fabermusic.com   fabermusic.com

someone to watch over me

Music and Lyrics by George Gershwin and Ira Gershwin

I love paris

Words and Music by Cole Porter

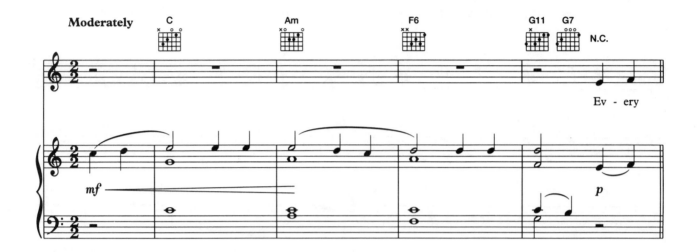

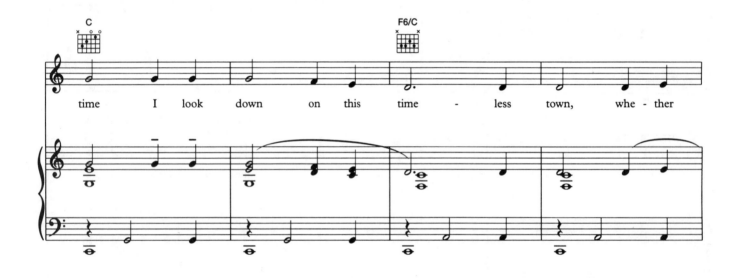

I love Pa - ris, why, oh why, do I love Pa - ris?

1. Be - cause my love is near.

2. Be - cause my love, be - cause my love is near.

summertime

Music and Lyrics by George Gershwin,
Dubose and Dorothy Heyward and Ira Gershwin

misty

Words by Johnny Burke
Music by Errol Garner

gone with the wind

Words and Music by Herbert Magdison and Allie Wrubel

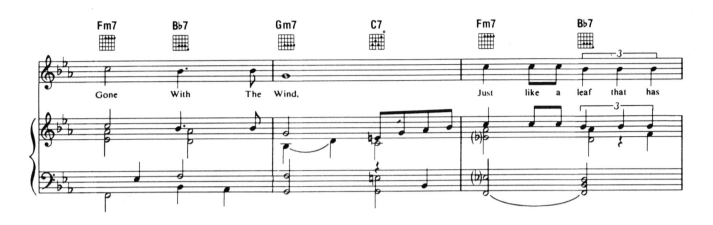

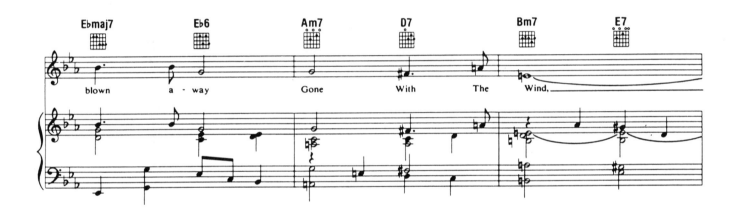

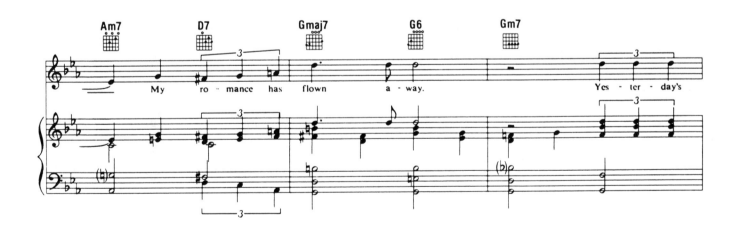

I can't give you anything but love

Words by Dorothy Fields
Music by Jimmy McHugh

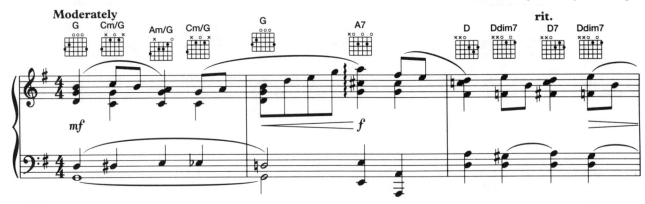

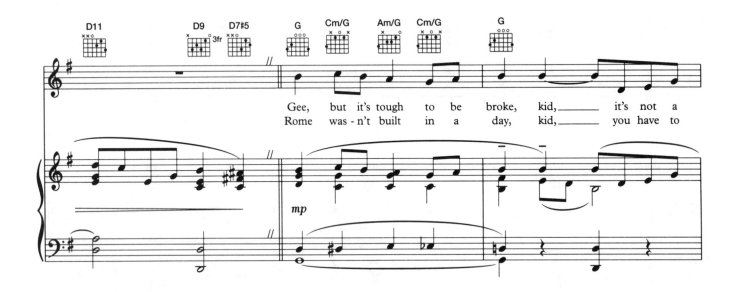

Gee, but it's tough to be broke, kid,_____ it's not a
Rome was - n't built in a day, kid,_____ you have to

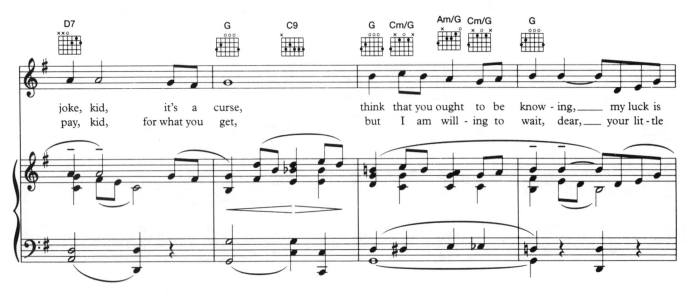

joke, kid, it's a curse, think that you ought to be know - ing,_____ my luck is
pay, kid, for what you get, but I am will - ing to wait, dear,_____ your lit - tle

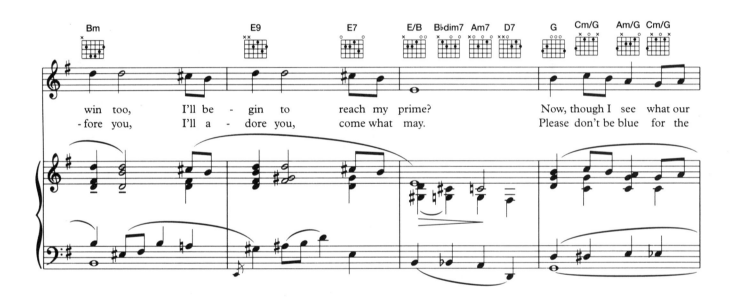

22

tenderly

Words by Jack Lawrence
Music by Walter Gross

I only have eyes for you

Words by Al Dubin
Music by Harry Warren

Are the stars out to-night? I don't know if it's clou-dy or bright, 'cause I on-ly have eyes for you, dear. The moon may be high, but I

mil-lions of peo-ple go by,_____ but they all dis-ap-pear_____ from

view,_____ and I on-ly have eyes_____ for

you._____ Are you you._____

love me or leave me

Words by Gus Kahn
Music by Walter Donaldson

Slowly (with feeling)

Verse (ad lib.)

This sus-pense___ is kill-ing me,_____ I can't stand___ _un-cer-tain-ty._____ Tell me now,___ I've got to know,___ Wheth-er you want me___ to stay, or go.___

31

these foolish things

Words and Music by Harry Link,
Jack Strachey and Holt Marvell

the very thought of you

Words and Music by Ray Noble

you do something to me

Words and Music by Cole Porter

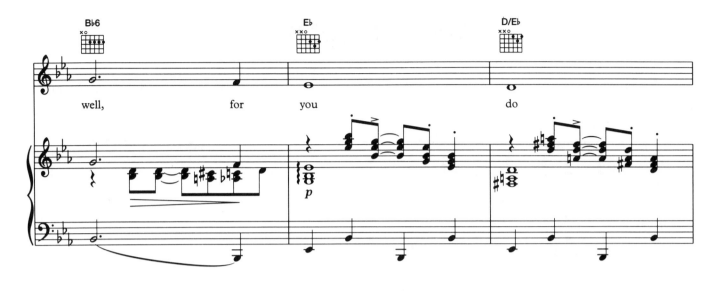

well, for you do

some-thing to me that no - bo - dy else could

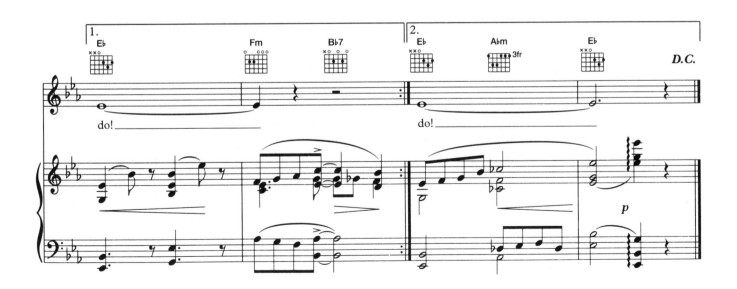

do! do! D.C.

I won't dance

Words by Oscar Hammerstein II, Dorothy Fields,
Otto Harbach and Jimmy McHugh
Music by Jerome Kern

mountain greenery

Words by Lorenz Hart
Music by Richard Rodgers

I've got my love to keep me warm

Words and Music by Irving Berlin

lullaby of birdland

Words by George David Weiss
Music by George Shearing

on the sunny side of the street

Words by Dorothy Fields
Music by Jimmy McHugh

I get a kick out of you

Words and Music by Cole Porter

one for my baby
(and one more for the road)

Words by Johnny Mercer
Music by Harold Arlen

all woman

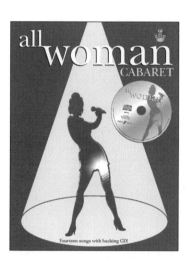

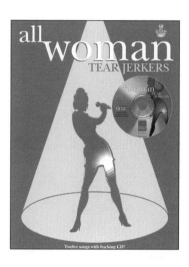

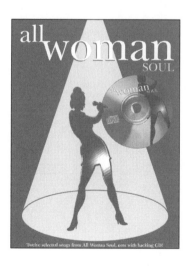

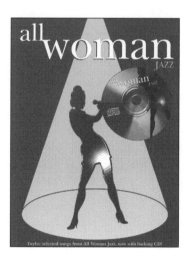

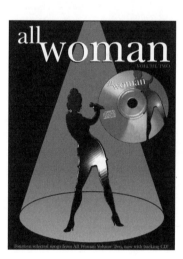

FABER *ff* MUSIC